Wizard Wagoo

written by Kaye Umansky
illustrated by Steve Smallman

The Story So Far ...

*Obby the Obbygobulum has been captured
by Giant Gong and the Gungees.
He has been taken to Gong's castle,
which lies beyond the Wild Woods and
up the Dizzy Mountain. Helped by
Myrtle the friendly turtle, the children
set off downriver on a raft. They get past
the rapids, but are spotted by the Gungees,
who throw stones at them and sink the raft.
The lift appears in the nick of time and
takes them home to safety.*

Now read on ...

Chapter One

Pip Leads the Way

"So," said Ben. "Who thinks we should go back?"

"Me," said Sam, firmly. "We have to find Obby."

"I didn't like the look of those horrible little Gungees," said Jojo, with a shiver. "And I hated the bit in the river. And I don't fancy meeting Giant Gong. But Sam's right. We can't stop now." Everyone looked at Mouse.

"Not today," Mouse said. "We can't go today. Not with Pip."

He flushed as he said it. Pip wasn't the only reason Mouse didn't want to return to the Wild Woods and everyone knew it.

"That's true," said Jojo. "We can't put Pip in danger. Mum would go mad."

Pip looked up from playing with his robot.

"I want to go!"

"No, Pip," said Sam. "You're too little.
This adventure is for big children."

"I am big," said Pip, crossly. And before anyone could stop him, he marched into the lift and reached for the magic button. He was just tall enough. As the children watched in horror, the doors closed …

and up went Pip!

Chapter Two

The Wizard's Cottage

The doors opened and out stepped Pip. He stood at the gate of a strange cottage, set amongst trees. It was painted in bright colours and had a **tall, twisty chimney.**

The gate opened, all by itself. Pip didn't stop to think. He simply trotted up the path.

The door was painted purple. The brass knocker was shaped like a dragon.

"Crocodile," said Pip, wisely. And he stretched out his hand.

"Stop, Pip!" came a shout from behind. Jojo came racing up the path with the others hot on her heels.

"What did Mummy say?" she scolded. "You mustn't go off on your own like that. Suppose the lift hadn't come back for us? You'd be all by yourself."

"Good," said Pip, sulkily. He got fed up with being treated like a baby sometimes.

"What's all the fuss?" came a deep voice – and the door opened. An old man with a long white beard stood looking down on them. He wore a purple robe and a tall, pointed hat. His eyes were blue and twinkling, like the sea on a summer's day.

"Wizard," said Pip, pointing.

"Sssh, Pip," said Jojo. "Don't point."

"But Pip is quite right, Jojo," said the old man.
He gave a little bow. "Wizard Wagoo, at your service.
Hello Ben, Sam and Mouse. Still on the trail of the
little Obbygobulum, eh?"

"How do you know our names?" gasped Ben. "Sir,"
he added, politely.

"Oh, I see a lot in my crystal ball. There isn't much
that goes on around here that I don't know. But come
in, come in. Don't be afraid. I'm on your side."

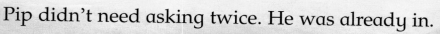

Pip didn't need asking twice. He was already in.

Chapter Three

Magical Gifts

"Oooh," said Pip, looking around curiously. "Funny."

The room was dark and shadowy. The walls were hung with strange charts. There were shelves containing little jars with mysterious labels. There was a work bench with bubbling test tubes giving off clouds of pink steam. There was a crystal ball and a wand hanging from a hook. Strangest of all, there was a tiny dragon with glittering green scales sitting on a wooden perch!

"A dragon!" gasped Sam.

"That's Dougal," said Wizard Wagoo. "Watch him. He's burnt a few fingers in his time. Say hello to our visitors, Dougal. No spitting fire."

Dougal spread his wings and opened his jaws. A tiny puff of green smoke came out. Sam moved back in a hurry.

"Want to play with Dougal," said Pip, moving forward. "Oh no you don't," said Mouse, grabbing his hand. "Behave, or we'll send you back home."

14

"Do you know if Obby's all right, Mr Wagoo?" asked Ben.

"I really can't say," said the wizard, shaking his head. "I've tried to trace him in my crystal ball, but all I get is mist. I suspect he's in deep trouble this time."

"But you're a wizard!" burst in Sam. "Can't you use a magic spell or something?"

Wizard Wagoo sighed. "I've tried every spell I know, Sam, but Gong has powers of his own. I've even tried setting off to the Dizzy Mountain myself, but it's hopeless. As soon as I start, the mists come down."

"Do you think the same thing would happen to us?" asked Ben.

"You won't know unless you try," said the wizard, simply.

The children looked at each other. One by one, they nodded. Even Mouse.

"We'll try," said Ben. Pip jumped up and down with excitement.

"I was hoping you would," said Wizard Wagoo. He pointed to the shelves. "I can't come with you, sadly. But I can offer you a little help. Take a look at the shelves. Each of you can choose something to help you on your quest."

"Even Pip?" said Jojo.

"Of course."

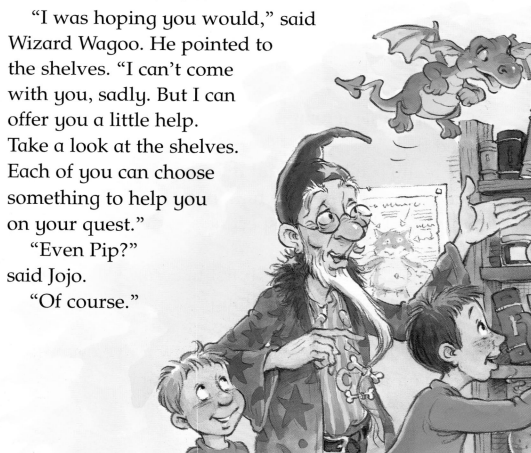

The children walked along the shelves, looking at the labels. What strange names!

"Slippery-Slide Cream," read Sam. "That sounds useful."

"Flying Dust," said Jojo. "I like the sound of that."

"Sneezing Powder," said Ben. "Great!"

"Strange Sweets," said Mouse, stopping at a big jar. "I've tried these. They turned me into a mouse, remember?"

"We remember," said everyone.

"What about you, Pip? What would you like?" asked Wizard Wagoo, busily unscrewing jars and shaking powders into little packets.

"I want Dougal," said Pip.

"No, Pip," said Jojo hastily. "Dougal is Mr Wagoo's pet. You can't take him."

"That's his choice," chuckled the wizard. "By all means take Dougal with you, Pip. He can show you the way."

There was a green blur. Then, suddenly, much to
Pip's delight, the tiny dragon was on his shoulder!

"He tickles," giggled Pip. He reached up and
stroked Dougal's tail. To everyone's amazement,
Dougal began to purr!

Purrrrr!

"Now, I have something else to give you,"
said Wizard Wagoo. "Follow me."

19

Chapter Four

Riding Tandems

Wizard Wagoo led the way outside. There, propped against the fence, were two bicycles with shiny handlebars and pedals and bells and everything.

"Where did they come from?" asked Jojo, eyes wide.

"They're not normal bikes," said Ben. "They're longer. They've each got two saddles, look. And extra handlebars."

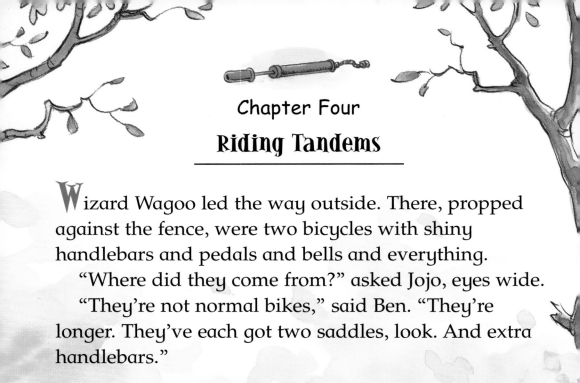

"They're called tandems," explained the wizard. "There are two sets of pedals as well. You'll go like the wind on these."

"How lovely!" said Sam. She couldn't wait to have a go. "I'll share with you, Ben. The twins can take Pip in their basket on the front."

Excitedly, everyone got on the tandems. Even Mouse was keen. Pip climbed into the basket and settled back, with Dougal in his lap.

Wizard Wagoo handed Ben and Jojo their little packets.
He gave Sam the pot of Slippery-Slide Cream.
Mouse's Strange Sweets came in a brown paper bag.

"Use them wisely," the wizard warned. "Don't waste
them. Take the path through the woods. If the mist
comes down, follow Dougal. Good luck. I'll be
watching in my crystal ball for as long as I can."

"Thank you," said everyone.

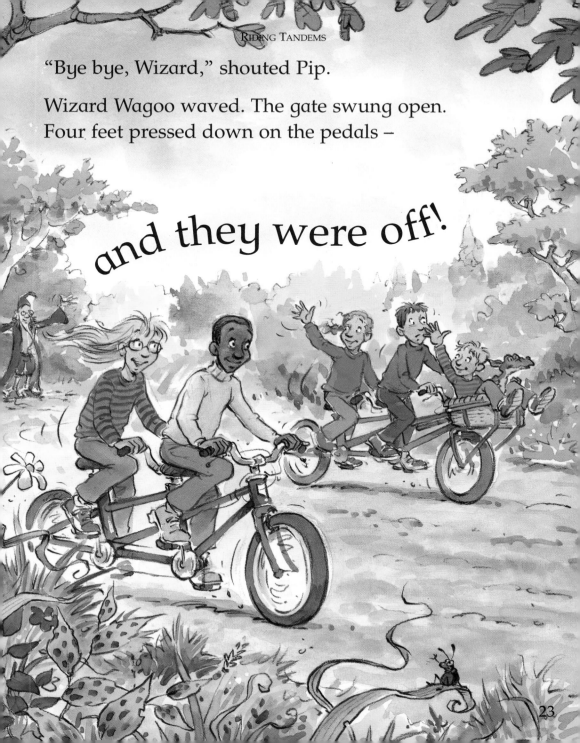

"Bye bye, Wizard," shouted Pip.

Wizard Wagoo waved. The gate swung open.
Four feet pressed down on the pedals –

and they were off!

Riding the tandems was wonderful. They almost seemed to move by themselves.

"Faster!" shouted Pip. "Faster!"

Dougal took off from Pip's lap and flew ahead, puffing out happy little puffs of smoke.

"What's that noise?" shouted Ben to Sam.

"What noise?"

"That buzzing noise. Coming from behind!"

Sam looked around – and her tummy turned over. Small, ragged figures, riding wicked-looking little black and yellow scooters were coming round the bend.

"Gungees!" screamed Sam.
"Pedal for your life!"

Chapter Five

Flying

Side by side, the tandems raced along the path. From behind came the sound of angry howls.

"They're catching up!" wailed Mouse.

Jojo risked a glance behind. It was true. She could see the face of the leading rider. She could see his teeth as he snarled.

"Right," said Jojo. "Time for the **Flying Dust**, I think!" She ripped open the little packet and sprinkled some dust over the handlebars. Then, she reached over and emptied the rest over Ben and Sam.

"**Oooooooer!**" screamed everyone
as all four wheels left the ground. Seconds later, both
tandems were flying up over the treetops. Dougal
streaked ahead of them, a tiny green dot against
the sky.

"Hold on tight, Pip. Don't look down!"
shouted Mouse.

But Pip was enjoying himself.
"Higher!" he shouted. "Higher!"

"Have we lost them yet?" shouted Ben.

Sam turned her head. Oh no!
Even as she looked,
the nasty little scooters
came bursting through
the treetops, buzzing
like angry wasps.

"They can fly!" screamed Sam.
"Oh, Ben! They can fly!"

The woods were now far below. Ahead, far away
in the distance, was a tall, snow-capped mountain.
Dougal was heading straight for it.

Suddenly, they plunged into a grey fog.

It swirled all around them,

blotting out everything except

the tiny, glowing shape of Dougal, who seemed to know exactly where he was going.

And then, just ahead, they saw a welcome sight.

It was the lift! It was floating in a sea of clouds.
Dougal hovered by it, puffing out smoke and pointing
to the open doors with one of his tiny wings.

The tandems flew right up to the lift and stopped,
hovering just outside.

Mouse snatched Pip from the basket and jumped into the lift, followed by Jojo. Ben and Sam did the same.

Sam hit the button, hard. As the doors closed, the tandems sank out of sight. The last thing they saw was a green flicker as Dougal sped away into the grey fog. The last thing they *heard* was the hateful buzzing sound of the scooters, getting closer!

"I feel sick," moaned Sam, staggering out onto the landing.

"Me too," groaned Ben.

"That was awful!" said Jojo.

"The worst yet," agreed Mouse, sagging against the wall.

"Fun," said Pip. "Want to go again!"